angel cues

Get Daily Angelic Alerts
From the Cards Inside

Book/Cards by JHBaldus

angel cues

Get Daily Angelic Alerts
From the Cards Inside

JHBaldus

Published By
JHBPressAustinTX

angel cues logo/cards/book
Copyright   JHBaldus   2016

ISBN 9780972521529

WHAT IS A CUE?

A cue is an alert/message given to someone by another. An example would be information given to a musician or a speaker/actor that it is time to be on the stage ...to perform! The cues/alerts in this book are given by a special group of angels each of whom has their name on their own ***angel cues*** cards.

These unsung angels are members of the entourage around the person to whom they were assigned - often from the person's time of birth until their death. I call this particular collection of angels "worker bee" angels. (I imagine them flying around and around their person in constant motion.) They are on call to assist their person 24/7- 365 days of the year. Their job is to make life easier, as well as teach their person how to feel emotions and learn human tasks. Not an easy assignment!

Regarding the existence of these, or any angels, we each have to decide for ourselves. I have a scientific background and have been a skeptic much of my life. At some level I probably knew angels existed but I called their input "inspiration" from my brain or in more gross terms my "gut" feeling. Not being able to knowingly "see" angels is a big obstacle to believing. A recent incident helped me acknowledge that something does NOT have to be seen in order to function/exist, however.

One day I was pouring wine samples at a grocery store when a little girl about age 8 came by and commented on the label of a bottle from which I was pouring. It was black and had a swirl of white around a "hole". (It was called "Black

Hole" wine.) She said, "They do not know if the black hole exists because no one has seen it." Then she smiled, waved and disappeared. I told myself, "It exists because the behavior of planets, stars and other bodies in the sky indicates it does." Guess I'm a believer in the power of the unseen after all!

ACKNOWLEDGMENTS

Once again, the genius known as Bill Benitez has taken something I created and turned it into a book available to all. Heartfelt thanks and blessings, Sir!

The original *angel cues* cards themselves evolved as I shared my ideas with others from strangers to friends to family. Their input was thoughtful and constructive. They loved the concept and the daily information via the cards.

Among those who made a distinct contribution early on is first of all, Sandy Hoag. She helped me translate the concept into reality. Then Grace Lalicatta, Vicky Stevenson, Jennifer Hill, Merrill Stanton, Philip (and Eugene) Holsworth, plus Billie Jo McAdams helped spread the word once the cards were available to the public. I send them all heartfelt thanks wherever they are.

To those who have encouraged me to continue providing access to the *angel cues* cards for anyone who wishes it ... thank you! I would never have thought to put the *angel cues* cards into a book without your insistence that there had to be SOME solution to the need for more physical card sets.

Now, you are able to make your own *angel cues* card set including coloring the heart on each of the cards any color you like. Enjoy!

CONTENTS

DESCRIBING ANGELS
What are angels, exactly?

Almost every person outside a cloistered "religious" group has their own description of what they think an angel is ... or is not. Many consider them emissaries from God. Others are not so sure.

Some consider the spirits of beloved (deceased) friends and family as angels. This was most humorously illustrated by Bill Keene in his cartoon strip named "The Family Circus". (The deceased grandparents were exhausted from constantly flying around trying to protect the lively children in the family from getting into trouble.)

Others believe that the ethereal entities, described in their religion's holy books as angels, belong to and protect only their religion's members.

Many folks have been assisted during an emergency by heroic actions from people unknown to them who then disappear and are never seen again. Often these rescued folks believe their heroes were actually angels.

Then there are those who received guidance from strangers who vanish once their directive is understood. I happen to fall into this category.

One late, snowy winter night, I was driving across farmland on unfamiliar back roads. Suddenly I saw a bright, blinking light across the field in front of me.

I rubbed my eyes in disbelief. The "light" was a figure hovering above the ground dressed as a Native American chief in full multi-colored headdress. In shock I looked down at the road and realized I was missing my turn and headed toward the middle of that field instead. Fortunately, I was able to get enough traction to make the turn. When I looked back, he was gone.

No one knew I was taking that road and I would not have been found for days as I was moving from one location to another. My guide had to be an angel!

And of course there are those who believe ethereal, unseen angels do not exist at all. However, they do usually honor earth "angels" - those people who are persons we wish to emulate because they are genuinely good individuals.

It does not matter if you believe in angels or not. These cards will bring insight into events and help you manage this experience we call "life."

WHAT ARE ANGELS? (whimsical answer)

Before discussing angels further an explanation of my ideas is probably in order here. Then I will explain how the the *angel cues* cards can help.

There are various analogies a person can make about the relationship of humans to God and the angels' role as well. I have come to believe that God exists and is totally composed of love and light/energy. However, I suspect God has to be neutral and non-involved directly in human events.

Please allow me to be whimsical to illustrate this. Let's imagine God as a dog breeder who has a litter of puppies to be trained. (Humans are the puppies in this scenario.) The puppies can do whatever they want because they have been given the gift of free will with no restrictions.

Now, puppies want to explore everything, including potentially dangerous situations. (That is not a stick - it is a venomous snake!) Since the puppies must learn by their own experience, God, personally, does not intervene as the puppy approaches the snake-snout forward. However, to help the puppy learn, God has authorized the puppy's trainers to intervene whenever appropriate -if only to lessen the damage.

God (and humans) call the trainers ... angels! Since being puppy/ human is very difficult, each one has their very own entourage of trainer "worker bees" angels. The goal of this enterprise is to help the puppy/humans achieve their potential and become totally competent and certified in the program called "Mastering Human Life".

Don't ask me how or why this program was started. I do not know. But we're in it, so with our trainer-angels' help we will complete this course of study. It may take many human lifetimes, however.

what are angels? jhb's prior awareness (subliminal)

Subliminal advertising (existing below the threshold of consciousness) is every-where. The other day I realized that angels are very good at it. Yes, I am talking about those ethereal souls that may /may not exist depending on one's personal per-ception/ experiences.

In my case they have been trying to develop my awareness of them since I was little because I resisted the idea of their existence . Gotta admit that I'm of the "if I don't see it, it isn't real," or at the very least "it has to be proved" school of skepticism.

For the first seven years of my life, I sat (wriggled) in our pew in my preacher grand-father's church sanctuary. I spent hours gazing at the sweet faces of the angels in the stained glass windows. And of course in Sunday school they were depicted in the Bi-ble stories. I even sang about them in the church choir.

Angel ornaments surrounded me on Christmas trees, in snow globes, in books and even on items such as "cherub" paper dolls. Plus there was jewelry and all the talis-man angel pieces, including the ones that hung on rear view mirrors of cars that said "Don't drive faster than your angel can fly."

As a student taking courses in art appreciation in college and then later in my trav-els, I was exposed to many renderings of angelic forms, usually with wings, in sculp-tures and paintings.

In fact, now that I think of it, the symbol of my secular, state university (Ball State University in Muncie IN) is Beneficence. Yep, an angelic figure with arms outstretched and wings spread symbolizing its and thus our mission ... to help others, especially students.

So, angels have always been a part of the fabric of my life. But since their meaning only registered subliminally, I had paid no direct attention to them until the day I started my research about angels. Then I learned how they were impacting my everyday life, even though I was oblivious to their efforts.

Also that was when I figured out that perhaps I owed my angels at least a nod of thanks. Plus,I probably had an obligation to share with others what I was learning about their ongoing helpfulness. So, now I am!

INTRODUCTION TO THE *angel cues* CARDS
What the angel cues cards are and their purpose.

The **angel cues** cards are a physical representation of the cooperative and ongoing connection between humans and their personal angels. The connection itself is at the soul level and lasts throughout the person's lifetime.

The purpose of these cards is to help us focus on the events of our daily lives. Reflection on those events will help us identify amazing elements of our lives we previously never noticed or appreciated.

By choosing a card at the start of our day we will watch for events related to the card's name. This watchfulness will improve our awareness and prepare us for learning experiences. Most folks do not like surprises - even good ones. So a card's angel alert may prepare us for all sorts of things to come.

These playing card style cards are not fortune-telling cards. They are to be used solely for the purpose of increasing our awareness of the interconnectiveness of it all as we remember the events of our daily lives.

Also, most of the time we humans go about our daily activities without giving any thought to the idea that a helpful entity unseen by us is might like to be acknowledged, even thanked for their assistance. So another purpose is for us to develop a ritual around using the cards that includes thanking our own personal angels for their assistance.

History of their development

As a medical person I had been looking for ways to help people deal with the tough events in their lives for quite some time. I especially wanted to learn non-medicinal ways to manage both physical and emotionally-related pain, which can feed on each other and raise the intensity of pain overall.

I was aware that day-to-day encouragement was needed as well. So I was searching for information that would provide physical evidence of ongoing support, particularly for the young and those who were on their own (no matter their age or circumstance). Possibly there was invisible support not known to the unaware? I really did not know.

As a child **I** had decided I should be able to do it "all" - alone. After all I was here on Earth "to learn a lesson" (per my grandfather's sermons). The emphasis was on the task being all mine. However, as life went on I acknowledged the assistance friends and family gave me but there were events they could not have engineered. Someone did but who were those entities?

One day a friend of mine told me he was "working" with angels. I stopped laughing when I saw he was serious. I began to look for explanations of who and what angels were beyond what had been taught in Sunday school. His wife firmly believed in angels and prayed for their individual help with various problems. My friend, himself, not so much. That was why my curiosity was piqued. If he had knowledge of something real, I wanted to learn about it.

I had heard about the famous ones, such as the Archangels Michael, Raphael, Fred, Sarah, and Jane. (just checking to see if you were paying attention.)

But there seemed to be others who impacted my life without my awareness. Oddly, there wasn't much general literature written about the "multitude" of others except as in groups, such as the Cherubim.

Finally, I found a book written about our individually assigned angels in our entourage of "worker bee" angels as I call them. I knew I had a Guardian angel but I had never heard about the individual ones assigned just to me. (Each of us has our own angels assigned to help us 24/7-365 days a year.)

Some of these angels serve all the way from our birth to our death. Others in our entourage come and go when needed for special occasions. But all show us how to be human with emotions and the ability to care about and for others. FYI They are not allowed to interfere with our actions (remember the "Prime Directive" from Star Trek?). But they can subtly guide us to help us learn how to become human. (It's a good thing.)

This book suggested that meditating on each angel's name was a great way to get to know our individual angels in our entourage. However, I was not about to try it ... collectively there were over 80 names! But I did write each angel's name, which represented its specific purpose, on its own plain white (half) index card.

One morning as I was idly shuffling the cards, I drew one. The angel name on it was appropriate for the day ahead of me. Curious, I began repeating the process every day to see what would happen. Surprisingly, the cards were relevant each time. Occasionally, the day's information was given very subtly, so I learned to pay attention. I didn't want to ignore any angel's guidance or alert (cue).

FYI The reason we each have our own angel group of "worker bees" is because the human experience is so complex. The angels contacting us the most are those trying to help us understand specific concepts. Thus, some have such names as Joy, Knowledge, Balance, Compliance, Beauty and Courage. We learn about emotions plus overall human behavior from them.

January 10, 2003 my granddaughter Katrina and I were making index card *angel cues* sets. My daughter Jennifer suggested I sell them. She even went out and bought little bags to put each set into. Not quite convinced, I needed to test market the cards. So I took them to work, to the store ... everywhere. I asked friends to "shuffle and draw" a card and I asked strangers. All were intrigued. However, the sets were too bulky. Eventually, I deleted those cards with angel names that seemed to be duplicates.

One day my brother, Philip, expressed concern about my having insulted those angels whose names were left out! So I sat down that evening and asked for guidance as I held each card and said that angel's name out loud. I did this with ALL of them! By the end of the day these 38 cards remained. Transformed from the original index cards, angel cues are now available to you as individual playing cards in this book.

SECTION ONE

ANGEL'S MISSION: to assist/teach their assigned person

concepts represented by the cards

List of 38 Cards-each identified by name/concept

ANGEL'S MISSION

The ***angel cues*** cards each represent cues/alerts from the angels named on them. The angels' "names" are the human emotions/tasks each is to teach their assigned person. Their assistance is ongoing.

LIST

ACCEPTANCE this angel cue usually appears when an action will be taken that cannot be refused. . OR information presented by you is approved

ACCOMPLISHMENT this angel cue often appears when you're attempting something new or controversial and the outcome is unknown

ADVENTURE this angel cue usually means plans will change unexpectedly and excitement ensues

BALANCE this angel cue usually means the day is overscheduled with too many obligations, possibly work- related, and needs to be rearranged to allow for some fun or rejuvenating activities, such as a short walk

BEAUTY this angel cue can represent almost anything, such as seeing something in nature, perhaps a double rainbow, or redecorating/buying new clothes or visiting the museum of art

BROTHERHOOD this angel cue can mean that folks having a common interest will be gathering OR some people unexpectedly learn of a shared interest

COMMITMENT this angel cue supports efforts to do something that was promised, either gladly or reluctantly

COMMUNICATION this angel cue indicates that it is time to convey difficult to understand information

COMPLIANCE this angel cue supports following expected procedure/protocol

COURAGE this angel cue often promises assistance with an unknown, or possibly even dangerous, activity

CREATIVITY this angel cue provides reassurance that the situation will be resolved appropriately even if how it will be is not yet known

ENCOURAGEMENT this angel cue indicates support for the activity /project

ENTHUSIASM this angel cue assists in building excitement for the future

FAITH this angel cue specializes in assisting with crises, especially family or emotional situations

FLEXIBILITY this angel cue assists in managing unexpected schedule changes OR requests from others

FRIENDSHIP this angel cue may help identify others who can or will behave like friends OR encourage friendly behavior towards others

GRACE this angel cue assists in acting with respect as well as kindness towards others

GRATITUDE this angel cue assists with expressions of thanks towards those who have helped accomplish a task or acted with kindness

HEALING this angel cue provides guidance for comforting someone who is physically hurt or emotionally bereft OR encouragement for one's own needs

HONESTY this angel cue assists when a situation needs to be clarified, usually due to a disagreement or misunderstanding

INSPIRATION this angel cue provides unexpected insight into how to resolve an issue OR a totally new idea may come to mind

INTEGRITY this angel cue is often present when a situation needs to be addressed with honor and right-mindedness

JOY this angel cue can be very subtle, surprisingly, and its presence may not be recognized until the day"s activities are reviewed OR there may be a happy feeling for a special reason immediately known

KNOWLEDGE this angel cue usually arrives when new information (unexpectedly) becomes available and clarifies a situation, or advances a plan

LIBERATION this angel cue occurs when an obligation has been lifted OR release from something is given by another

PATIENCE this angel cue assists when a task at hand is tedious, or complicated OR someone new comes in and everything done so far has to be re-reviewed

PEACE this angel cue often comes when important events with no clear outcome are occurring (everyone is upset) and provides reassurance that all will be okay

PLANNING this angel cue assists when unexpected opportunities present themselves and need to be included OR deadlines are fast approaching and it needs to be determined who will do what /when in order to complete the project on time

PURITY this angel cue assists with having no hidden agenda or motive to improve things for oneself at the expense of others OR in other words, thinking and acting unselfishly

REDEMPTION this angel cue helps us identify an opportunity to right a wrong we did in the past OR to give someone else the chance to do the same for us

RELAXATION this angel cue supports "indulging" in relaxing activities so much so that that they should be put on the calendar as appointments

RELEASE this angel cue advocates "letting go" of such emotions as anger/ guilt/ pride/sadness/worry and will assist in that effort

SELF-ESTEEM this angel cue creates opportunities to counter negative feelings such as doubt, concern regarding one's abilities, feeling unworthy or being bullied

SIMPLICITY this angel cue encourages keeping it simple if for no other reason than complicated situations are exhausting and not conducive to creative thinking

STRENGTH this angel cue supports endurance training for activities that require physical strength OR the concept of "give me strength" meaning extra patience to endure nonsense could be what the angel cue is really interested in

TENDERNESS this angel cue suggests subtle demonstration of caring is likely OR quiet unexpected gestures could suggest appreciation

TRANSFORMATION this angel cue expects major changes OR unexpected visual changes OR internal/emotional changes

TRUTH this angel cue supports reality (as each perceives it) will be understood/shared

SECTION TWO

How to get angel cues/alerts

Interpretation Guidelines

Copies of each card (one per page)

jhb's brief comments about every card (on the next page)

HOW TO GET ANGEL CUES/ALERTS

The ***angel cues*** cards are imbedded in this book. If you do not want to cut them out of the book, then close your eyes and randomly open the book to the ***angel cues*** card section. The page you choose will have the name of your card for the day on it. When you open your eyes ... you will have your alert.

If you prefer to use actual ***angel cues*** cards, then create your own set by cutting them out of the book. (See Section Four for instructions.) Once your set is made, you may shuffle and draw a card whenever you like. No rigid schedule is necessary since your angels are always around you. However, many people have found that it is best to establish a routine so that they do not forget to take consistent advantage of their angels' assistance.

My routine is to shuffle the deck and draw a card while my morning coffee is brewing. My cousin prefers to do this in the evening before going to bed - something about getting her angel primed for the next day.

Keeping the cards in the same place is helpful. One of my friends stores hers in a pretty box next to the toothpaste in her bathroom. Another friend keeps them near his car keys. I have mine in a cool box on a dresser. Keep them wherever you wish, just so it's easy to remember where they are.

INTERPRETATION GUIDELINES

The card chosen for the day can be interpreted as information coming to you (the drawer) OR it may be that you will use the info for another.

For example, once Sarah drew the **angel cue** card Beauty. It was Mother's day, and Sarah was going to visit her mother. She had been undecided what to take as her mother did not want a gift. After drawing the card Sarah decided to take beautiful, cut flowers in an unique vase to her mother.

The key is for you to observe and remember the events of your day. Matching the cue's "name" to the day's events is half the fun. At the end of the day, review its happenings and you will discover support the angel provided.

Either you will notice what was brought to you OR you will realize what you gave to another during this time. Both are valid and valuable and both can happen in the same day. (Thank your angel for the help it gave you, please.)

Best of all. Once we pay attention to our day, we will remember anything we learned. Thus we will have expanded our learned human behavior. Yeah!

However, if you are puzzled whether the angel cue's info actually did relate to your day, do not be concerned. Sometimes it takes awhile before the full meaning of a prior day"s events becomes clear. If you remain unsure after looking at the situation from all sides, do not worry about it. The next time you draw the same card, the new day's events might be less confusing.

Acceptance

ACCEPTANCE

Acceptance can mean many things, but there seem to be two major ways it can be intended. It could mean that some action or idea you are receiving from others makes sense to you. Conversely, it could suggest that others find you or an idea you are presenting agreeable to them.

Self-acceptance is also a relevant possibility. Hurrah for any day we find out information about ourselves that makes us understand ourselves better! For example, I always waited until the last minute to do paper work, or to study . I hated myself for that tendency but could not seem to change it.

Having changed schools approximately every other year due to Dad's work, I never was anywhere long enough to be properly diagnosed as ADD. Also, as many girls are, I was a daydreamer more than an agitator like the boys. It was only after I had my Masters that I was properly diagnosed ... at age 55! Now I take a small dose of Ritalin when I need to focus.

I finally accepted that I was born this way just as many others in the US are. It is a genetic construct that has actually served us well as a nation. We are children of immigrants who were not satisfied with the status quo. The knew there had to be a better way to live. Thus, we are a nation of souls continuously striving to improve our world.

Accomplishment

ACCOMPLISHMENT

Accomplishment is usually fairly clear to identify. It most often means you will complete a task or goal. I see it as an encouraging card to get. Frequently it shows up when I am dreading some task. It is nice to know that the angel's support will help make the effort a success.

It also can mean that someone else will complete something for which you will give them applause/recognition for their success.

Almost anything large or small can be applauded- from safely persuading the cat to get into the carrier to go to the vet - to having one's ideas accepted by a prestitious group at an international conference. The idea is to recognize the amazing events that occur in our lives and give recognition to the angels who helped us. A heartfelt "thank you" goes a long way, I understand.

Adventure

ADVENTURE

Adventure can mean just about anything that is exciting and,or unexpected. I find it often means challenges are ahead but I try to think of it as my angel telling me it is "on it" and everything will be handled. In other words, pay attention and be flexible. And at the end of the day there may be quite a story to tell. Or something that could have been overwhelming turns out fine.

Another person may tell you on this day about their plans and you encourage them to follow their instincts that will result in an actual adventure,such as kayaking class 5 rapids.

Balance

BALANCE

Balance often shows up when one's schedule for the day is overloaded or overbooked. But not necessarily with work. Take a look at your schedule to see if there is too much of one type of activity and not enough of something else. For example maybe there is no time for lunch. Or you're planning nothing but indoor activities when it happens to be the first day of spring and is a lovely day. Rearrange your schedule where you can, so you will have a more pleasant as well as productive day.

If you are working with someone who seems "out of sync", you may notice they are too heavily involved in just one type of activity . You might suggest they look at their schedule and include something else like a walk after lunch.

FYI - Hyperfocusing on a project is when folks often get overbooked. Breaking a project into smaller tasks could help them see where to plan a change of activity in their schedule. That activity should refresh their mind and body. Ultimately, they will be more productive.

One day years ago I drew the card "Beauty". I was really sad and saw no beauty anywhere. Then I saw a flower in a booklet with the following saying beside it, "When we find balance, we find beauty." That saying spoke both to balance and beauty. It is on my desk today.

Beauty

BEAUTY

Beauty is something that seems so obvious, but often is not because not all beauty is big and bold, such as a sunrise or a sunset. Also, beauty is not always noted because we are so absorbed in everything else, we miss it.

Furthermore, the old saying that beauty is in the eye of the beholder is very, very true. Probably the perfect example of that is an old episode of the TV show Rod Sirling produced, "The Twilight Zone." In it a group of aliens of another planet were bemoaning the ugliness of one of their young women. They had just told her there was no other way to make her presentable than for her to have plastic surgery. Then she turned around so we (the viewers) could see her. She was a stunning blonde (Earthling-looking)!

So, when you get this card slow down, look around and enjoy your world. Then you may decide to do something that will beautify your corner of it, or you discover something that is just what you needed for that purpose. Also someone may bring something to you that is unexpected and beautiful. Express your appreciation and then enjoy.

Brotherhood

BROTHERHOOD

Brotherhood is a very versatile term. It can be broad such as the "Brotherhood of man" or refer to one's siblings. But most of the time it refers to folks from groups who gather together for the same purpose at a scheduled place and time.

Members of each group consider themselves part of that brotherhood. They identify with and belong to that group as well as many others. I know of a group of neighbors who all shop at the same grocery store at about the same time and are delighted to see each other there each week.

Often their similarities are what bring each group together and their interests keep them involved with and supportive of each other. When I get this angel's card it usually means I will see someone whom I care about but haven't seen for a long time. Or I will join a group of people who are gathering together spontaneously and will find a common interest with them.

I also pay attention during the day, because I may meet a new person and discover we have the same/multiple interests. One time I met a person my age, who had also worked in the medical field, had lived in my home state and was writing a book at the same time as 1 was on a related subject. Brotherhood established!

Commitment

COMMITMENT

Commitment usually refers to keeping a promise. You are being reminded of your promise when you pull this card. You have an obligation that the angel doesn't want you to forget it could even be a promise you made to yourself.

And of course the promise may have been initiated by another person to meet you at a particular time and place to conduct business with you. So, commitments may come from others. Promises go both ways.

On a day when I had no plans/obligations I pulled this card. I was puzzled why I got it. A few minutes later the phone rang. The exterminator was on his way for his quarterly visit. I had completely forgotten. He kept his commitment but I did not remember mine. My angel was right!

Another time, I pulled this card and remembered that I was invited to an evening business meeting. I really did not want to go, but I did not want to upset the convenor of the meeting. So, encouraged by my angel, I went.

Good that I did. I caught up with business contacts and friends I hadn't seen in months. I thanked my angel for the prompt.

Communication

COMMUNICATION

Communication is an especially encouraging card/angel. Since so much of our existence is based on our ability to express our thoughts and needs, it usually shows up for me when something very difficult needs to be conveyed. I usually see it as a sign that the day I draw the card is a good one for me to attempt to make my ideas known. It often means the person who will receive my info is in a receptive mood. That always helps when the subject is complicated.

I'm not the only one who looks at it this way. One time a doctor pulled the card, and promptly headed for a hospital phone saying," I need to make a difficult call, now."

If there is no call/e-mail/tweet/facebook posting you need to make, the communication may come to you from someone else. Be prepared to explore new ideas that may be coming to you. Any way it happens, communication is an all important ability. Use it well and remember to thank your angel!

Compliance

COMPLIANCE

Compliance most of the time refers to following the rules. They can be someone else's rules/requirements. Or they can even be one's own such as "I will not start the car unless the handbrake is on."

Where the angel's support can be encouraging is when compliance involves multiple activities, has complicated steps or involves doing something one really does not want to do.

For example, in order to work as a person pouring wine samples one has to get certified by the state alcoholic commission after passing a test given by them following their mandatory class. The location is difficult to find and class times put an applicant on the road smack in the middle of rush hour. So drawing that card on the day of the class helps reassure the applicant that it will all work out just fine. Really.

On the other hand, if one is responsible for overseeing an activity being done by someone else, receiving this card helps one feel that the person they are observing is going to perform all the tasks correctly and there will be no problems. Whew!

Courage

COURAGE

The angel of courage is one of the most demanding members of your angelic entourage - while being one of the most intensely supportive of you! It urges you to attempt things you ordinarily would rather not.

With its support you will find yourself achieving the impossible, or at least what you used to think was not doable by you, although many people do it all the time. Others will see you attempt new things and will gain reassurance that they too can do what seems impossible, if they at least try.

Let me be clear, however, I am not talking about heroic activities or known physically unsafe ones such as trying to ride a bull at a rodeo. Heroic activities just happen without pre-planning. A person acts on instinct, although to be honest, their angels help them of course. But the event is not one that will be repeated, hopefully.

I am talking about ordinary events. For example, even though I have been a paid professional speaker/instructor, I am shy at social events sometimes. However, when I get that card and not wanting to "disappoint" my angel of courage, I make myself attend that day's social function. When I mingle with other guests, I always run into friends or make new ones. So, good times!

Creativity

CREATIVITY

Creativity is all around us, but when the angel comes forward it means you need to pay special attention because an idea you get may have major impact on you and others. And of course, it could also mean that someone else is bringing a creative idea to you that should not be dismissed.

Sometimes ideas come so quietly that we tend to either ignore them altogether or not give them our full attention. Most ideas do not come fully formed, but just as an interesting concept. Only when it is pondered and turned around or various versions are tried does it evolve into a full-blown viable project worthy of your time and energy.

When I ran out of the original angel cues card sets I realized I did not have the resources to make more. It made me sad to think their info was no longer available and I felt as if I were letting people down who really needed them.

Then after I published my first book, it struck me. I could put the cards in a book that folks could buy. And the book could be configured in such a way that people could cut out each card and make their own set! I took my idea to the designer Bill Benitez, who loved the concept and created this/my book!

Encouragement

ENCOURAGEMENT

Encouragement consists of positive words/deeds that help someone continue with their task or project. These can be from you to another, or from another to you.

Notice if the timing of getting this **angel cues** card helped you push on to meet the deadline of your current project.

One time a friend asked me to go to work for him which I would have loved to do. He was such a great mentor that a school of business was ultimately named after him at a Midwestern university. However, I was getting ready to work on a project in another country. He was disappointed but his directive to me was to go on as I had planned and "Follow your star."

I always remembered his words and never tried to keep a good employee from moving on to a new learning situation. Also I made sure they were accompanied by a positive recommendation from me.

Enthusiasm

ENTHUSIASM

Enthusiasm is a positive expression of excitement and approval over others' plans or achievements. They will be pleased over your happy response.

In turn enthusiasm can be for what you are experiencing or about to experience. This angel often shows up when you need an extra energy charge for what you expect your day to bring. This is an advantageous card when you are expecting to have to persuade /sell others on a product or idea of yours. Others are more likely to become interested in the subject if you are excited about it of course.

I find it much easier to proceed with an idea if someone else whose opinion I value and trust likes it. When I first came up with my plan of putting these angel names onto cards that people could use for daily information/support, I showed them to friends and excitedly asked their opinion of the idea. All liked them and some made suggestions that were very helpful.

One friend went so far as to help me figure out how they should look. We decided on a playing card style and size since people are used to games in which they pick a card for the purpose of the game. Fortunately this card style made the process of recognizing an angel's assistance more easily understood and thus more readily acceptable to those unfamiliar with the concept of angelic assistance. The cards in this book are those same ***angel cues*** cards.

Faith

FAITH

Faith is the conviction that you are on the right path and that positive results will be a result of your efforts. Although they may not be the results you planned you expect/trust they will be to your benefit. In other words, you "trust your gut," or your instinct.

This angel shows up most often for me when I am unsure of the outcome of my situation. The effect of getting the angel's reassurance is that I relax and become more trusting that whatever happens is for the best.

Before my first book was published, I took a draft copy of it to a business meeting. A lady who liked it asked to be notified when it became available. She wanted to give it to her sister. Several months after its publication I found the lady's business card. I debated whether to call her, but finally did since I had drawn "Faith" that day.

She answered the phone but said it was not a good time and hung up. I got the impression she had changed her mind so I threw the card away. Fifteen minutes later I got a call from her. She had been delivering her husband to the airport, but now was exactly the perfect time for her to hear the book was available because she needed the information that was in it!

Flexibility

FLEXIBILITY

Flexibility is important but getting this card does not necessarily mean we need to run off for an extra session of yoga. Being mentally flexible helps as we go through our daily routines and various distractions that arise.

This angel comes forward for me when there is a particularly unsuspected event that is going to occur. Being alerted to the possibility keeps me from being so focused on my plans being set in concrete.

One time I almost got myself fired because my work station was arbitrarily changed to a location that was detrimental to me physically. The young manager was looking at the location from an aesthetic viewpoint, forgetting that a person was going to have to work in the new space. Another manager came up with a compromise that was workable, but I got written up for voicing my initial objection.

The next day I wrote a letter explaining I was not challenging his authority to make assignments. But the fact that I would have been off work sick as a result of his decision seemed counter-productive. Ultimately the manager showed flexibility himself. He accepted my explanation and also apologized.

Friendship

FRIENDSHIP

Friendship represents the people who make our lives worthwhile. This angel often comes forward to alert you to someone whom you may not think is a friend but actually is. They may have done something that benefits you and you will just today find out about it.

Or perhaps there is an unexpected gathering of people who are your friends and good times ensue. Maybe you meet a stranger, then discover you are from the same part of the world, love the same sports teams and you develop a friendship.

In other words, those who are friends look out for your interests and you do the same for them. Many times these are folks you are not certain you like when you first meet them, but as time goes on you begin to trust each other and ultimately become friends.

Your angel is encouraging you to notice who is behaving as a true friend to you and reminding you to do the same for others. The world is full of new friends just waiting to meet you and enjoy good times with you.

angel cues

Grace

GRACE

Grace is the ability to maintain a pleasant, accepting manner in what may be an unwanted change in circumstances without whining. I get tickled at this description because this does describe my friend, Grace. And sometimes when I get this card, she calls me that very day.

Most of the tme when I get this card, there is an aggravating situation that occurs. Knowing that there is no point in getting my blood pressure up, I try to stay as calm as possible. I get faster resolution to the problem if I project a cool, adult persona.

And of course I respond better to another when they are also doing the same. Hopefully they are able to control the situation and achieve a reasonable solution that both of us can live with. Regardless it is up to me to control myself and give in to the inevitable if that is necessary as long as it isn't harmful or illegal.

Being in a state of grace is always commendable. It may be tough to achieve sometimes, but with your angel's help....

Gratitude

GRATITUDE

Gratitude, or at least verbalizing "thanks", is often not done in the stress of everyday life. However, not only do humans appreciate the effort, but so do the angels. There is the concept that the thanks does not need to be excessive, but done with true appreciation for the effort made by another is a major factor in keeping any relationship in good shape. Recognizing true thoughtfulness shows good character and certainly encourages more of the same from others. So be sure to show gratitude to all those in your life.

Accepting gratitude is sometimes a difficult thing to do. It can become embarrassing. But if the person saying "thanks" is genuinely pleased, then that makes your effort all the more valuable. We should not do things for others in order to earn their gratitude, but because it makes us feel good to help them. I believe that is why the angels enjoy helping us.

Accepting kudos for doing one's job is difficult. But if it makes your bosses happy, then be gracious about it. Others would love to have your situation.

Healing

HEALING

Healing consists of words and deeds performed to assist others who are wounded physically , emotionally and/or mentally. Often when I get this card, I meet someone who needs comfort but I did not know their troubles. I try to do what I can by at least listening to them.

Kind words and actions from others also can help heal me when I need it. So if someone approaches me I try to accept what they are offering as graciously as I can. One time not too long after my son died of AIDS (it was the early days of the epidemic) I attended an event being held in a bookstore. I was speaking with a nice lady selling bookmarks.

The conversation turned to my son. I described him as a talented rock and roll musician, with a great head of hair and green eyes, who was 6'1". The lady said that he was 6'2". I started to correct her, but she looked me in the eye and said,"He says, he was six foot two!" Shocked, I smiled at her and walked away. She was trying to help me and there was no arguing with her. And after I checked with his dad, I found out she was right.

Hearing from my son via that lady was indeed a healing event. Bless her.

Honesty

HONESTY

Honesty is when a person relates what they think about someone's ideas or actions. It can be a good thing, because we all need another's perspective on situations at times. And as we also know, it can be a destructive behavior because if it is negative it is based on the outlook of the person being honest and may not be helpful at all. Or it could be very useful. It all depends on the information as well as the intention of the person being "honest."

This angel has the tough job of mentoring you and also fortifying you at the same time. The main thing to remember is that other's opinions are exactly that. . . their own opinions. And by your angel's coming forward and alerting you, you can put your shield up and be prepared. Hopefully that won't be necessary, however. The feedback could be quite wonderful.

Just do not allow honesty to be an excuse for bad behavior on your part or anyone else's. Stay alert.

Inspiration

INSPIRATION

Inspiration is all around us. But I have found that when I get this angel's card, there is something I need to notice that I might have ignored before. Also it is encouraging, especially when we are stuck, to know that we have support in our quest for useful ideas.

Frequently an idea comes to me while I'm a taking a nap or am asleep at night. (I make myself wake up enough to write the idea down on the notepad kept on my bedside table.) And of course sometimes I hear, see or read something that gives me an idea.

Often the ideas I pay the most attention to are those that build on something I've already discovered. No invention or concept is created in a vacuum of course. We subconsciously take a perspective we can use and refine it or revise it entirely while giving credit to its source when we know it.

Musicians make their living by remembering lots of musical notes. However, they may find themselves accused of stealing another's creation. Often they do not realize there is a problem until they get told about it, usually in very harsh terms. Unfortunately for the original artist, musical plagiarism is very hard to prove. Copywriting their work can help, though.

Integrity

INTEGRITY

Integrity assists us as we refuse to take a short-cut that is unethical or use a dishonest method of doing something. It also helps as we resist saying something about another that is untrue or unkind. In other words, we are honest, trustworthy, care about others and want the best for all.

Not only does integrity refer to us, but it reassures us that a person or a company we are going to be dealing with is trustworthy with high standards of performance. They have our best interests at the core of their service.

When you are surrounded by persons of integrity you can trust that the information they bring you is correct. You can rely on them. Therefore, you can act with confidence based on their information.

Joy

JOY

Surprisingly, joy can be a very subtle one. I always think it should be alerting me to something huge, such as a BIG bucket of gold coins on my front porch when I get home. (Hasn't happened, yet.)

However, lasting joy builds from the small day to day events that give us reason for smiles - such as a butterfly coming to the window, or the polite nod of the head from a stranger. Often the recognition of joy results from finding the sweetness in our day that helped make life worth living.

Also, we may have done something for another that we did not think was significant, but indeed may have brought great joy to them. The angels' like to help us do good things for others, too.

Finding joy in unexpected circumstances is fun as well. The other day I got a phone call from a former employee. He was coming to town to give a presentation about his new invention at a conference. He wanted me to see it and to take me to lunch. I accepted of course. Wonder if we will recognize each other after 30 years?? We did!

Knowledge

KNOWLEDGE

Knowledge comes in many forms from many sources. When I get this angel's assist it often relates to things someone should have told me. So, I try to pay particular attention throughout the day when I get this card. Great information is all around us. We just have to choose what is important to us.

Of course knowledge also refers to what we have learned and keep in our experience bank. That is the type of information we share with others. And hopefully what others will share with us.

One reason this angel may be contacting you is to remind you that information or knowledge even of ordinary things can change. In other words, maybe you do need to watch that exercise commercial that seems so annoying. It may encourage you to try something that is vital for your health.

Liberation

LIBERATION

Liberation can be achieved when you give others info that relieves them of a burden. The burden could be emotional, financial, personal, mandatory responsibility, historical, physical, or something else.

In turn when someone gives you information or takes an action that relieves you of a burden, even if the burden is self-imposed, you need to be aware that burden is gone and you have been liberated (freed).

However, sometimes a person does not realize they have been under the strain of a burden. That may be why the angel has come forward to alert you that you have been liberated, because sometimes the burden is so subtle that you did not realize what was happening.

Or it could just be that no one had informed you so your angel came forward to help you become aware of the good news.

angel cues

Patience

PATIENCE

Patience is something none of us ever have enough of, particularly those of us in the US. Genetically we are an impatient peoples. Unless our ancestors were dragged here on a slave ship, we are progeny of folks who were impatient with the way things were working out in their home countries and decided to try somewhere else (that they knew little about of course).

Our angel of Patience has its work cut out for it. Basically it tries to encourage us to calm down, slow down, look around, then plan a logical approach to whatever is going on. Once that is worked out then follow the plan. (Ha.) As I said your angel of Patience has quite a job.

Sometimes, your angel is trying to help you assist others with pacing their efforts to a good outcome. Part of that outcome is to not be rushed, so as not to become annoyed/irritable at not having enough prep time.

In addition to encouraging planning ahead and leaving enough extra time in case obstacles occur, relaxation techniques can contribute to the desired outcome. Remind your protege', or yourself for that matter, to take deep breathes (exhaling through your mouth), listen to soft music and perhaps even take a nap before leaving for a presentation.

angel cues

Peace

PEACE

Peace is a state of mind that we all want to achieve as often as possible so we can devote our time to various interests. When we are at peace we remain calm, not worried or anxious. I have found that my angel shows up when I am totally obsessed with something that is not going well. I am in a negative state of mind that is not productive and my blood pressure is rising.

Thankfully after I get this card, I am able to calm down and entertain the idea that a positive resolution of the problem is in the works and will become known to me soon. The old adage "All in good time" always comes to me. It is hard not to be in control of my loved ones' lives, and I have to remember I cannot be responsible for everything in their universe. Peace is what I need - along with perspective!

Sometimes the peace angel is not coming to help me, but to assist me with calming another and showing that person I care about them. Or Peace wants me to realize that others are trying to help me even though I might not know about it. Peace reassures us that loving souls are all around us—literally.

Planning

PLANNING

Planning is almost self-explanatory. To get anything done that has more than one step, you have to plan, or should. Folks who cannot plan need assistants (actual people) to help them. I am a planner almost to an extreme. I suspect I have a touch of OCD in me, which has probably been a good thing.

However, when I get this angel's card, it often means that a major project is coming up, such as planning an event with my family /friends, or collaborating with the team at work on a new assignment.

Regardless, my angel gives me extra support and so will yours.

Purity

PURITY

Purity is a self-monitoring angel that helps you control your thoughts and actions so that you do not demonstrate unkind or unwanted ideas or behavior. Everything we do, think or say spreads out into the world and influences others, known or unknown. And if any of it is negative, I have read that It fuels or creates more negative thoughts and actions in others.

It is a big responsibility for you and your angel. And it can be confusing. The easiest way to remember what purity means is to think of it as being totally unselfish in thought, word and action. When one is unselfish they are thinking positively about others no matter who the other is or how they behave. This is the basis of the Golden Rule.

When the angel of Purity shows up, I do a mental check to see if I am unconsciously thinking/planning something that is selfish, unkind, thoughtless or self-centered. Then I make sure it doesn't happen during the day ahead.

Purity is a state of being we can ask our angels to help us strive to achieve.

angel cues

Redemption

REDEMPTION

Redemption is definitely a two-way angel. It represents words or actions taken by someone to repair damage done to another by word or deed. It is a genuine effort to try to gain forgiveness from the aggrieved person in hopes that the relationship can be restored to at least a level where both parties can exist together.

Any time I get this angel's card I try to figure out whether I need to be redeeming myself or someone else is trying to work things out with me. Often it is a total puzzle until I think what I can do or someone comes up to me.

Incidentally, sometimes it is not a person seeking redemption. I just got a settlement check in the mail from a major company that had lost a class-action suit that I had forgotten I was part of.

When this angel shows up It always is an interesting day.

Relaxation

RELAXATION

Relaxation - it doesn't seem like we need an angel to make us aware of the need for it. But we do. As go-getter people, we program ourselves with so many tasks and obligations that we literally do not leave any time to relax or even think about it. And if we do, it usually involves other members of our families. Taking time just for ourselves is still considered self-indulgent (or a guilty pleasure) by many although there are all sorts of studies that say "alone time" is critical to our emotional and mental health.

Thus the need for our Relaxation angel to remind us of our obligation (to ourselves if no one else) to stay emotionally and mentally healthy and to make time in our schedule so "alone time" can happen. It may be no more than 20 minutes but it definitely needs to occur.

Also, this angel might show up to remind us to monitor others, including our children, to be certain they get some "me" time. Our associates should get some unobligated time and of course our significant others should have the same without any discussion on our part whatsoever.

So, if the relaxation angel shows up, take the message seriously!

angel cues

155

Release

RELEASE

Release refers to letting go of something that has been bothering you. Often when this card shows up new or reassuring information about an issue or person will be received. Sometimes the info is unexpected and this angel's alert is to encourage you to pay attention and not miss it. Once the info arrives and you are satisfied with it, then you are able to release your prior concerns.

Or possibly with nudging from this angel,you may be the one communicating something to someone else that helps them release a concern of theirs. We never know sometimes.

Release also can refer to an obligation that may be hard to meet. For example a person may have volunteered to take someone to work in the immediate period after that person's car was totaled. Then the volunteer's schedule was changed and it takes an extra trip to meet that obligation. Once the accident victim has obtained another car, the volunteer can be released from their obligation.

Self-Esteem

SELF-ESTEEM

Self-esteem is a busy angel for many people. We can decide at any time that we are not a person others will approve. There rarely is a reason to think or feel that way . However, as humans we tend to decide we are "not worthy" because we set impossible expectations for ourselves.

We are more uncertain when we are young. We do, however, tend to improve our self-confidence and thus self-esteem from our achievements large or small as we forge through life.

Nonetheless our angel often has to work overtime to alert us to information that indicates we are truly special and to remind us to respect the intentions of those who wish to acknowledge us.

By the way, your angel may alert you to someone whose self-esteem would receive a boost if they received acknowledgement from you. Possibly a mentoring effort from you might be an option.

Simplicity

SIMPLICITY

Simplicity is one of the most difficult concepts for humans to understand. We tend to embellish everything we do or say. Making something simple seems like cheating. We just have not put enough effort into something if it is simple to say, do or operate.

Just look at all the concerns that were expressed when Twitter was launched. The idea of only using 140 spaces to get an idea across in writing seemed absurd at the time. Then it turned out it could be done . Succinct expression became a communication standard.

Simplicity encourages us not to make things unnecessarily complicated. I usually get this card when it is my first attempt at putting together a project or I have scheduled myself to run all over the place that day. I stop and take another look at what I am doing and usually wind up paring it down. I'm not as stressed as a result.

When working with others I try to give ideas that will not only clarify the project but make it more achievable. Often they will have simplying ideas for me once they realize simple is best. Simple is easier to explain and do.

FYI I really valued this angel's support as I edited my writing.

Strength

STRENGTH

Strength as represented in the angel cards does not necssarily mean physical strength. It can, and sometimes does. However, one of the fellows who was testing the original cards for me said "It means 'give me strength' (as in give me patience)". He was right.

After I get this card, I can become and remain calm during some of the most exasperating/frustrating situations ever. I must confess it is partly because every time I think of how he said that, I have to laugh.

Strength of character is another interpretation I like. It is easier to work with people who have strength of character. When you meet one, you probably find yourself trying to think how you can work with them in the future.

Tenderness

TENDERNESS

Tenderness, the angel, is alerting you to be aware of/pay attention to any kind words or behavior that shows someone cares for you. It also is alerting you to possible opportunities to show caring kindness to others.

This angel is assisting you to not only receive tenderness without scoffing but to give tenderness without overwhelming the recipient. A light manner is appropriate when showing tenderness as you acknowledge others and thank them for their contributions to your world.

This angel reminds you it is helping you identify those opportunities.

Transformation

TRANSFORMATION

Angel cues may not have the same impact or weight each time. Sometimes they represent something major. Some times they alert us to consider or notice something more subtle.

Example: One day I drew "transformation." I was off work that day so I knew the "transformation" was not happening there. 1 had just gotten a haircut, so it probably was not referring to my appearance. Puzzled and curious I absent-mindedly tried to open the vetical blinds to the patio. The control stick would not turn. So, I forced the blinds across the rod so I could see out.

Later that day my daughter came over and helped me anchor a sheet to the rod to help shield the large windows from the sunlight. After the sheet was wrapped over the rod it looked really cool -like an old-fashioned valence.

It had "transformed" the look of the window. Wonder where I got the idea???

Truth

TRUTH

Truth is not the same as honesty. It stands alone. We know that everyone has their own version of "the truth". And when we get to heaven, we will learn "the" truth about everything that happened in our lives. Some of it we will already know and other parts we may not.

Truth, our angel, helps us determine what is true, or correct, versus what is not, so we have a frame of reference for how we wish to respond to the situation in front of us.

More importantly, our truth is facilitated by our angel. We wish to be trustworthy and respond appropriately in order to help others. Our angel is letting us know, assistance is at the ready. We have support in uncovering what we need to know.

SECTION THREE

Evaluating the impact of the cards' alert on your day

Q&A with jhb

Epilogue

EVALUATING THE IMPACT OF THE CARD'S ALERT ON YOUR DAY

TIPS for recognizing the fun and insight you got from today's *angel cues* card

BEGINNING of the day (plans)
Are you going to / did you change something after drawing today's card?

END OF THE DAY (review)
Was there someone who needed your "help"? Or wanted to help you with something?

THE REST OF THE DAY'S STORY
Anything else you noted because the angel's cue focused your attention?
Did you change your mind about anything after you read the angel's cue?

DON'T FORGET to thank this angel for it's help …. YIPPEE!

Q&A with jhb

Q   Can anyone else use my cards, or will that confuse my angels?

A   Anyone can use your cards. But always shuffle them thoroughly when you use them again. For that matter, suggest the borrower shuffle the cards before using them so their angels' energy is on the cards.

Q   Do I have to keep the angel cues cards in a special box?

A   You do not. However, I do recommend keeping them in the same place, so you will remember where they are. If you do have a box or container that fits them, they will stay cleaner if inside it rather than lying around loose. Also, you will be less likely to lose one of cards.

Q   May I draw more than one card each day?

A   You may draw as many as you wish. I find that drawing two gives me enough challenge for my upcoming day. More then that is distracting for me. Most folks find that one ***angel cues*** card draw is enough for each day. Remember you are watching for that *angel's cues* throughout the whole day.

Q   What happens if I forget to use the ***angel cues*** cards every day?

A   Nothing will happen. The ***angel cues*** cards are a visual communication tool for use by you and your angels. The angels will still be helping you even if you are not in communication via these cards.

EPILOGUE

A few weeks ago, I was telling an old friend about my plan to put the ***angel cues*** playing card set into book format. This friend used to own a well-regarded bookstore, so was pleased with the idea.

As our phone conversation continued, she began looking for her set of the cards. (She had recently moved.) Happily she found them and chose the angel cue card "planning". As we ended our conversation she said, "Well, don't know what this card means. I haven't done any planning so far today."

After we hung up, I realized she had just spent quite some time, while talking to me, figuring out how she could coax one of her (adult) children into complying with an unwanted but necessary medical test. She had come up with a very workable plan. Surprise! Her angel had done exactly what it promised to do...assisted her with planning.

This scenario illustrates the value of reflecting on the day's events. When we notice what actually happened, we often are quite pleasantly surprised. The angel's assistance can be quite subtle but is always meaningful.

SECTION FOUR

How to make your own playing card set

How to laminate the cards (including resource info)

HOW TO MAKE YOUR OWN PLAYING CARD SET

If you prefer to have a playing - card style set of the cards, you can cut out each card from the pages of this book, then - shuffle and draw one from the set you just created.

A complete set of cards is easy to make. Start by cutting each of the 38 angel cues cards pages out of the book. (Each page with an angel cues name on it has a vertical line along the spine to follow when you are cutting it out of the book.)

Also, the name page has a solid line outline around the name of the card. Just cut around the outlines carefully and your cards will have an angel's name on one side and the ***angel cues*** logo on the other side.

FYI The original ***angel cues*** cards were laminated to keep them looking good. Note: you can laminate the cut-out cards using pocket laminating kits from office supply stores or the Internet (info on page 195).

HOW TO LAMINATE THE CARDS

Laminating cards like these should not be complex. The important thing is to purchase a laminating product that is simple and inexpensive.

During our current search, we found an Avery Self-Adhesive Laminating Sheets packet that comes with 50 sheets in the 9 X 12-inch size, more than enough for several sets of cards. The Avery products are available on Amazon for $14.98 (and from other sellers for as little as $8.99). Just go to Amazon.com and search for Avery Self-Adhesive Laminating Sheets if you wish to buy from them.

The important thing is to purchase a simple product with self-adhesive, so it's not necessary to buy a laminating machine.

Warning, you may have so much fun laminating the cards (directions are easy to follow) you may find yourself looking around the house for other things you can laminate!

ABOUT THE AUTHOR

The author is a medically trained, Masters - prepared individual who has an interest in nonmedical activities that help people with their reality. In 2002 Ms Baldus created a practical method of receiving cues/alerts sent to us by those ethereal souls we call ... angels!

She created a playing card style set of cards called ***angel cues***. A person could chose a card randomly from the ***angel cues*** set in the morning. The word on the back of the card (an angel's name/ purpose) would alert them about how to prepare for that day's events. The cards were laminated - to make them last forever.

After making over 700 sets of cards (38 cards/set) the author sold out of them. Finally, to meet requests for more sets, the author decided to create this book for the purpose of making ***angel cues*** cards available within. (Each of the cards has its own separate page that can be removed from the book and the card itself cut out.)

Since her retirement from the medical world, she has been writing a blog on current events. Her first book was "*P.S. To The Beyond: Communicating With (departed) Loved Ones.*" published by JHBPressAustinTX in 2014 and currently available on Amazon and Kindle.

Ms Baldus is an empathetic, well regarded, and effective hypnotherapist credentialed by the American Board of Hypnotherapy. She has her practice and resides in Austin TX, USA to be near her grandchildren.

She may be contacted through the publisher, JHBPressAustinTX@gmail.com.